Ten Po
about A

ex libris

Candlestick Press

CW01511628

Published by:
Candlestick Press,
Diversity House, 72 Nottingham Road, Arnold, Nottingham NG5 6LF
www.candlestickpress.co.uk

Design and typesetting by Craig Twigg

Printed by Bayliss Printing Company Ltd of Worksop, UK

Original Selection and Introduction © Anne Harvey, 2013
Additional poems selected by Katharine Towers, 2024

Cover illustration © Hilke MacIntyre, 2024
http://hilke.macintyre-art.com

Candlestick Press monogram © Barbara Shaw, 2008

© Candlestick Press, 2013 and 2024
Second edition, revised 2024

ISBN 978 1 913627 36 2

Acknowledgements

The poems in this pamphlet are reprinted from the following books, all by
permission of the publishers listed unless stated otherwise. Every effort has been
made to trace the copyright holders of the poems published in this book. The
editor and publisher apologise if any material has been included without
permission or without the appropriate acknowledgement, and would be glad to be
told of anyone who has not been consulted.

Thanks are due to all the copyright holders cited below for their kind permission:

Christine Webb for 'Aunt Em' © Christine Webb, from *After Babel*, (Peterloo
Poets, 2004). David Higham Associates for permission to reprint both 'Aunt
Sue's Stories' by Langston Hughes, from *Collected Poems of Langston Hughes*
(Alfred A Knopf Inc., 1994) and 'Dora' by Charles Causley, from *Collected
Poems 1951 – 2000* (Picador, 2000). 'Aunts' by Virginia Graham is reprinted
from *Consider the Years* (Persephone Books, 2000), www.persephonebooks.co.
uk. 'The Niece', by Martin Armstrong, is reprinted by permission of Peters Fraser
& Dunlop (www.petersfraserdunlop.com). 'A House of Mercy' by Stevie Smith,
from *Collected Poems of Stevie Smith* (Penguin, 1972), is reproduced by
permission of James & James Publishers, Executors of the Estate of James
MacGibbon. 'Aunt Julia' by Norman MacCaig, from *The Poems of Norman
MacCaig* (Polygon, 2009), is reprinted by permission of the Estate of Norman
MacCaig. Moniza Alvi, *Split World: Poems 1990 – 2005* (Bloodaxe Books, 2008)
www.bloodaxebooks.com. John McCullough, poem first appeared in this
pamphlet, by kind permission of the author. Joyce Sutphen, *First Words* (Red
Dragonfly Press, 2009). Reprinted by kind permission of author.

Permission for additional poems cleared courtesy of Dr Suzanne Fairless-Aitken
c/o Swift Permissions swiftpermissions@gmail.com.

Where poets are no longer living, their dates are given.

Introduction

"There is something in the relationship between aunts and their nephews and nieces that is quite unlike any other," wrote essayist Robert Lynd adding, "Looking back I can see that there is nothing but good to be said of aunts".

As an aunt myself I find that very encouraging, especially as aunts often get a very raw deal in literature. Tony Lumpkin in Goldsmith's comedy *She Stoops to Conquer* says, "To be sure Aunts of all kinds are damned bad things" and it seems that Richmal Crompton's William Brown and PG Wodehouse's Bertie Wooster would agree with him. Some very judgemental, tight-fisted and quite extraordinary aunts appear in these books, and are matched by countless other gorgons such as Lady Bracknell in *The Importance of Being Ernest* and the dreaded Aunt Reed in *Jane Eyre*.

The aunts of my childhood are well-remembered: Big Auntie Bessie, who liked to warm her backside at the fire, lifting her skirt… snobby Auntie Constance, who liked to buy even her buttons in Harrods… Great Aunt Ada, who however lavish the set tea-table always found something missing. In the words ending Virginia Graham's warm and loving tribute, all those "nigh-forgotten, soon-remembered aunts".

Anne Harvey (1933 – 2022)

We're grateful to Anne Harvey who selected the poems for the first edition of this title. This updated edition is dedicated to her memory.

The Aunts

I like it when they get together
and talk in voices that sound
like apple trees and grape vines,

and some of them wear hats
and go to Arizona in the winter,
and they all like to play cards.

They will always be the ones
who say "It is time to go now,"
even as we linger at the door,

or stand by the waiting cars, they
remember someone – an uncle we
never knew – and sigh, all

of them together, like wind
in the oak trees behind the farm
where they grew up – a place

I remember – especially
the hen house and the soft
clucking that filled the sunlit yard.

Joyce Sutphen

Aunt Julia

Aunt Julia spoke Gaelic
very loud and very fast.
I could not answer her —
I could not understand her.

She wore men's boots
when she wore any.
— I can see her strong foot,
stained with peat,
paddling the treadle of the spinningwheel
while her right hand drew yarn
marvellously out of the air.

Hers was the only house
where I lay at night
in the absolute darkness
of the box bed, listening to
crickets being friendly.

She was buckets
and water flouncing into them.
She was winds pouring wetly
round house-ends.
She was brown eggs, black skirts
and a keeper of threepennybits
in a teapot.

Aunt Julia spoke Gaelic
very loud and very fast.
By the time I had learned
a little, she lay
silenced in the absolute black
of a sandy grave

At Luskentyre.
But I hear her still, welcoming me
with a seagull's voice
across a hundred yards
of peatscrapes and lazybeds
and getting angry, getting angry
with so many questions
unanswered.

Norman MacCaig (1910 – 1996)

Dora

My last aunt, Dora Jane, her eye shrill blue,
The volted glance, the flesh scrubbed apple-clean,
Bullets for fingers, hair cut like a man,
Feet in a prophet's sandals, took the view
That work was worship; kept a kitchen share
In this her book of very common prayer.

She never called me Charles. Instead, the name
My father went by: Charlie. Who brought home
The war stowed in his body's luggage; died
In nineteen twenty-four. The strong wound bled
Unspoken in her heart, no signal tear
Disburdened on a waywardness of air.

One tale she prised from childhood. Prised again.
A brother and two sisters. How they ran
To the high field, through the tall harvest sea,
The stolen matches for a summer game.
As it was born, each pretty painted flame
Matching the sun's fire. And how suddenly

The youngest was a torch, and falling, falling,
Swathes of her long hair, and her burned voice calling.
Indifferent, the sun moved down the day:
The boy, my father, beating hand to bone
On the hard flame that struck a breath away
And turned a body and blood to a black stone.

Caught in her trap of years, Dora still told
Her tale, unvarying as granite. Held
Life at arm's length. And there were lovers, though
The clear blue gaze killed questioning. Revered
The tarot pack, fortunes in tea-cups. Feared
Nothing when it was time for her to go;

Half-smiled at me as a sentimentalist.
The biscuit-tin clock thumping by her bed
Placed so that she could see the day drawl by.
Our only death, said Dora, is our first.
And she turned from me. But her winter eye
Spoke every word that I had left unread.

Charles Causley (1917 – 2003)

Aunt Sue's Stories

Aunt Sue has a head full of stories.
Aunt Sue has a whole heart full of stories.
Summer nights on the front porch
Aunt Sue cuddles a brown-faced child to her bosom
And tells him stories.

Black slaves
Working in the hot sun,
And black slaves
Walking in the dewy night,
And black slaves
Singing sorrow songs on the banks of a mighty river
Mingle themselves softly

In the flow of old Aunt Sue's voice,
Mingle themselves softly
In the dark shadows that cross and recross
Aunt Sue's stories.

And the dark-faced child, listening,
Knows that Aunt Sue's stories are real stories.
He knows that Aunt Sue never got her stories
Out of any book at all,
But that they came
Right out of her own life.

The dark-faced child is quiet
Of a summer night
Listening to Aunt Sue's stories.

Langston Hughes (1902 – 1967)

My Other Auntie

has a crew cut and moves fast in a crowd.
She guffaws at the idea I'm the first queer

in our family, points to old photos' borders –
a blur that's the animal of her face escaping,

a starburst that's her glass beads diverting
the light. I murmur her name on the phone

in my student flat and she ambulances over,
a flurry of sunflowers and let's-sort-this-out.

My body is an airport I snivel. *Men land
on me and fly away.* She lists ex-girlfriends,

tells me stories where she screws up too –
when to scoot, how to say no. How to gleam.

for Maria Jastrzebska

John McCullough

Presents from My Aunts in Pakistan

They sent me a salwar kameez
      peacock-blue,
         and another
   glistening like an orange split open,
embossed slippers, gold and black
      points curling.
  Candy-striped glass bangles
     snapped, drew blood.
  Like at school, fashions changed
     in Pakistan –
the salwar bottoms were broad and stiff,
     then narrow.
My aunts chose an apple-green sari,
  silver-bordered
     for my teens.

I tried each satin-silken top –
  was alien in the sitting-room.
I could never be as lovely
     as those clothes.
  I longed
for denim and corduroy.
  My costume clung to me
     and I was aflame,
I couldn't rise up out of its fire,
  half-English,
     unlike Aunt Jamila.

I wanted my parents' camel-skin lamp –
  switching it on in my bedroom,
to consider the cruelty
     and the transformation
from camel to shade,
  marvel at the colours
     like stained glass.

My mother cherished her jewellery –
   Indian gold, dangling, filigree.
         But it was stolen from our car.
The presents were radiant in my wardrobe.
   My aunts requested cardigans
         from Marks and Spencers.

My salwar kameez
   didn't impress the schoolfriend
who sat on my bed, asked to see
   my weekend clothes.
But often I admired the mirror-work,
   tried to glimpse myself
         in the miniature
glass circles, recall the story
   how the three of us
         sailed to England.
Prickly heat had me screaming on the way.
   I ended up in a cot
in my English grandmother's dining-room,
   found myself alone,
         playing with a tin boat.

I pictured my birthplace
   from fifties' photographs.
         When I was older
there was conflict, a fractured land
   throbbing through newsprint.
Sometimes I saw Lahore –
         my aunts in shaded rooms,
screened from male visitors,
   sorting presents,
         wrapping them in tissue.

Or there were beggars, sweeper-girls
  and I was there –
      of no fixed nationality,
staring through fretwork
      at the Shalimar Gardens.

Moniza Alvi

The Niece

Miss Prudence, careless of her name,
Allowed Jim Sykes, her latest flame,
To lure her to the Dog and Duck;
And there it chanced, by sheer ill-luck,
Her Aunt, Miss Emma Apsley-Bing,
Rather a go-ahead old thing,
Had just popped in, resolved to pry,
With modest but observant eye,
And so discover what the blazes
People *do* inside these places,
And there among the glass and glitters
She sat enjoying gin-and-bitters.
Spying her niece she muttered 'Gee!
How very awkward this will be!
No sociological explanation
Will ever meet the situation.'
And, feigning not to notice Prue,
She racked her brains for what to do.
Miss Prudence, leaning on the bar,
(You know what these young people are),
Fell, as she spotted Auntie Emma,
Into a similar dilemma;
For 'Fancy meeting *you* in here!'
Would gall the sensitive old dear,
While 'Auntie, have the next on me!'
Might fail to strike the proper key.
And so, with perfect coolness, backed
By worldly wisdom and a tact
For which too much cannot be said,
They simply cut the other dead.

But now, whene'er they chance to chat
Of that and this and this and that,
They stare into each others' eyes
Furtively, with a wild surmise.

Martin Armstrong (1882 – 1974)

A House of Mercy

It was a house of female habitation,
Two ladies fair inhabited the house,
And they were brave. For although Fear knocked loud
Upon the door, and said he must come in,
They did not let him in.

There were also two feeble babes, two girls,
That Mrs S. had by her husband had,
He soon left them and went away to sea,
Nor sent them money, nor came home again
Except to borrow back
Her Naval Officer's Wife's Allowance from Mrs S.
Who gave it him at once, she thought she should.

There was also the ladies' aunt
And babes' great aunt, a Mrs Martha Hearn Clode,
And she was elderly.
These ladies put their money all together
And so we lived.

I was the younger of the feeble babes
And when I was a child my mother died
And later Great Aunt Martha Hearn Clode died
And later still my sister went away.

Now I am old I tend my mother's sister
The noble aunt who so long tended us,
Faithful and True her name is. Tranquil.
Also Sardonic. And I tend the house.

It is a house of female habitation
A house expecting strength as it is strong
A house of aristocratic mould that looks apart
When tears fall; counts despair
Derisory. Yet it has kept us well. For all its faults,
If they are faults, of sternness and reserve,
It is a Being of warmth I think; at heart
A house of mercy.

Stevie Smith (1902 – 1971)

Aunts

Children, when you have gone your several ways,
and have sought the long days'
happiness, and the night's elusive dream,
incredible as it may seem
you will turn, at some moment, like thirsting plants
to your aunts.
   Now, aunts are not glamorous creatures,
as very often their features
tend to be elderly caricatures of your own.
Aunts use eau-de-cologne
and live in rather out-of-the-way places,
and wear pointed white shoes with laces
tied in a neat bow.
   Oh, I know, I know!
   Nevertheless I maintain
that when you are old enough to learn pain,
are acquainted with sorrow, and know what fear is,
your aunts will not seem nearly such drearies.
   You'll see,
believe me!
   When you've broken off your engagement and want to hide,
you will go to Aunt Beatrice at Ambleside.
When the charwoman falls down dead,
Aunt Edith will give you a bed.
When your heart breaks, as hearts sometimes do,
Aunt Constance at Looe
will feed it on Cornish cream and philosophy,
soothe it with strawberries for tea;
and when, with the dew still behind your ears
you set forth to conquer wider spheres,
I do not think you will get much further the first night
than Aunt Maud in Shanklin, Isle of Wight.

Oh, yes, children, aunts are kind
and quite resigned
to the fact that you will not go near them for years,
and then bring them your tears.
Although at your tender age
you resent their neglect of the Stage,
their inability to differentiate between jazz and swing,
and their poor reactions to Bing,
the day will dawn when they will rise up like rocks,
sheltering you with their long imprimé frocks
and cornflowered hats worn at such hopeless slants –
your nigh-forgotten, soon-remembered aunts.

Virginia Graham (1910 – 1993)

Aunt Em

There was Aunt Em. She was earth mother:
baked her own bread, made porridge
lemoncurd gravy biscuits
sewed worn sheets sides to middle
gave her youngest sister hints about
sex, sang contralto in the chapel. Shirts
and china rose brilliant from her soap-foamed
hands, more gnarled each year. She sat down
seriously in the library, choosing
her books with pursed lips, nodding
at her pencilled list, the fragile bun
of her hair quivering, skewered
with pins. Fifty years she ruled
kitchen and family with loving
labour and sharp-eyed reproof. I see her
eternally brandishing the blade
of the handle-less breadknife, making a point
in some argument, as she cut the bread
on returning from chapel, with her hat still on.

Christine Webb